E … nent

Presence, Word, Gift, Community

Ian Silk

Teacher and Mission Enabler

GROVE BOOKS LIMITED

RIDLEY HALL RD CAMBRIDGE CB3 9HU

Contents

Acknowledgments

Thank you to all members of my family, especially my wife Alison and sons Geoff, Stu, Rob and Andy; also to all friends at Grove and in the other Christian communities I have had the privilege to be a part of and learn from.

In loving memory of Karin, an encourager

Note

The biblical translations in this book are from the New International Version unless specified otherwise.

First Impression February 2025

ISSN 0262-799X

ISBN 978 1 78827 447 0

What is Encouragement?

1

Introduction

What is encouragement in common experience, and where is it needed?

I asked some friends: 'heartfelt, sincere words to build up,' 'a word ministry to the church that addresses discouragement, meeting a need or solving a problem,' 'deeds of kindness.' So is it words, or actions, or both? Is there a difference between giving encouragement and showing mercy? Someone said encouragement does it with words while mercy rolls up its sleeves and gets its hands dirty. Someone else said education and encouragement go naturally together, the one lovingly drawing out and building with what is within and the other putting in what is needed to confront our fears.

Encouragement is an *intentional* ministry of word and action that aims to make a difference to people in body, mind and spirit. 'Encourage' is 'in-courage'—giving support, confidence or hope to a person or a group of people. 'Without this gift of encouragement we die. Bereft of it life becomes unbearable and full of misery.'[1]

I wonder, is encouragement a home thing or an away thing? In order to encourage others should we stay where we are or do we go somewhere else? People came to visit John Newton in his home and were encouraged and he also wrote to them from his home—although letter writing could also be understood as a form of visiting.[2] Elizabeth Fry went to visit people nobody else visited, in prison; she was an away encourager and yet it seems her own home was often full of people who needed encouragement—family members, friends, church members.[3] Home or away? Perhaps the answer to 'where' is 'everywhere!'

People who are great encouragers may more often be known for something else; their public role is an outward expression of a ministry of encouragement that is more behind the scenes. It is only when we hear more of their life story that we realize just how much God has used them in other ways too. One of my favourite examples of this is Billy Graham, who as well as being the voice of the Lord on stage in Harringay in Britain in 1954 was also known in India as 'Angel of Mercy' because of his practical help for those affected by a tidal wave in 1977.[4]

The enigma of encouragement—is it a quiet gift or does it make a sound? Yes! Is it private or public? Is it a home thing or an away thing? Yes! Is it words or is it deeds? Yes! Is it for a moment or is it for a lifetime? Yes, it can be all of these things. 'When we encourage, we're quite like God.'[5]

Pause for Thought

'Without.................I would not be where I am today'—try filling in the gap.

Barnabas, the Son of Encouragement

I wonder who first encouraged Barnabas, such that he became such an encourager himself? We are not told. Like so many encouragers, Barnabas seems to appear with gifts of encouragement to give, gives them, and then melts back into the background leaving a trail of encouragement in his wake. Encouragers are towers of strength who build other towers of strength—patiently, deliberately, consistently: comforters who comfort others with the comfort they themselves have first received; investors in people whom they perhaps will never actually see with their own eyes; releasing the gift of encouragement to spread unseen through communities. Barnabas is a bridge-builder, whose bridges stretch far further than he could ever have imagined. Because of this son of encouragement we have Paul who himself became an encourager, we have John Mark who wrote a gospel that has travelled through space and time, and we have a church full of Gentiles, possibly you and me.

Barnabas has the gift of *alongsideness*. He comes alongside the new church in Antioch; seeing evidence of the grace of God at work he rejoices at the new and slightly scary thing that is happening, encouraging them to remain true to the Lord with all their hearts (Acts 11.23). But he does not stop there, because encouragement is an active ministry that takes initiatives. Barnabas' world-changing act is to get Paul alongside the Antioch Christians and they both pour in the teaching at just the right moment; ministers are gifts of encouragement. In Antioch, we are told, the disciples were first called Christians. Something came together there—encouragement was on the loose! And a moment, or rather a season, became an unstoppable movement that continues to this day all over the world.

We all have the ability to encourage others and so let loose a flood of blessed consequences in and through those we encourage. Barnabas is a great example of this and of the cost we sometimes have to pay. The results ripple out across the world though we may never know it. So then, whether it is by word or dynamic action, whether by offering a listening ear or hospitality, or by visiting the needy or supporting those who fail, let us be encouragers who by so doing learn to build the kingdom and grow the church.[6]

Pause for Thought

Can you think of other examples of 'sons and daughters of encouragement' where a moment became a movement?

Scriptural Engagement

Paraklēsis

The word for encouragement in the Greek text of the New Testament is *paraklēsis* and an encourager is a *paraklētos*. The Holy Spirit is by centuries-old Christian tradition the paraclete, so it may be helpful to think of God the Holy Spirit as God the *encourager*. But what sort of encourager? One study of the role of paracletes in Greek writings prior to John's gospel points out something surprising: 'The *paracletes* are not portrayed as advocates in the court but as persons striving to use their connections...to persuade the jurors to decide in favour of their client before the trial has even commenced.'[7] I wonder then if Barnabas, that son of *paraklēsis*, was not in fact exercising a ministry of 'holy brokerage' that reflected particularly clearly an important aspect of the Holy Spirit's own powerful ministry of connection and mediation among God's people? This sort of encouragement from God through others can really make a difference!

We can read the parts of Scripture which talk about the paraclete with a number of aspects of encouragement in mind: 'Do not let your hearts be troubled,' says Jesus. 'Trust in God, trust also in me...I will ask the Father, and he will give you another *Encourager* to be with you for ever—the Spirit of truth...All this I have spoken while still with you, says Jesus. But the *encourager*, the Holy Spirit, will teach you all things and will remind you of everything I have said to you...My peace I give you' (John 14, my translation).

Translators and interpreters need to make choices. *Paraklēsis cannnot be translated into one single English word.* Encouraging, counselling, exhorting and comforting are some of the options, but which one should we use in a particular context? In Luke 2.25 it is often translated 'consolation' but it is much more than that. Simeon, along with so many others, has been waiting for *encouragement,* which he now discerns to be embodied in the child Jesus that he cradles in his arms: 'Now there was a man in Jerusalem called Simeon, who was righteous and devout. He was waiting for the *paraklēsis* of Israel, and the Holy Spirit was upon him...' (Luke 2.25).

This word *paraklētos* has a background in the Old Testament: '*Encourage,* encourage my people, says your God' (Isaiah 40, my translation). The Hebrew equivalent is *Menachēm*: One who comforts, encourages. 'Your rod and staff encourage me' (Psalm 23, my translation). You comfort, console, guide, strengthen, restore, shepherd me.

> God is our encourager—
> God the Father is our encourager
> God the Son is our encourager
> God the Holy Spirit is our encourager.

Praise be to the God and Father of our Lord Jesus Christ, the Father of compassion and the God of all encouragement, our Encourager in all our afflictions, causing us to be able to encourage other afflicted ones by passing on the encouragement with which we have been encouraged (2 Cor 1.3–5, my paraphrase).

We hear of the gift of encouragement in Paul's Letter to the Romans: 'We have different gifts, according to the grace given to each of us. If your gift is prophesying, then prophesy in accordance with your faith; if it is serving, then serve; if it is teaching, then teach; if it is to *encourage*, then give *encouragement*; if it is giving, then give generously; if it is to lead, do it diligently; if it is to show mercy, do it cheerfully' (Rom 12.6–8).

Prophesying, serving, teaching, encouraging, giving, leadership, showing mercy…a perfect seven and a rainbow spectrum of gifts in ministry. And encouragement is right at the heart of the seven. It is a facilitating gift in relation to all the others. So if someone's gift is to encourage, let them encourage! Release the encouragers in the church and in the world, for where there is encouragement all the other gifts and ministries will be enhanced. I think it is interesting too that in the list in Romans 12 encouraging sits neatly between teaching and giving and there is surely an overlap! Certainly, when we begin to think about why encouragement works in practice, we find we cannot dissect this rainbow spectrum—in Jesus Christ prophetic action, words of teaching, deeds of giving and alongside compassion are not separated. Encouragement reaches out in both directions. It embraces a whole ministry of wholeness and hope.

Does encouragement have anything to do with personality? There is good news for those of us who perhaps feel we are more introvert: we can be encouragers. Eugene Peterson sees *paraklēsis* as something that happens quietly, in conversations, informally; less noticed perhaps than pulpit preaching or classroom teaching. He links the gift of encouragement with the gift of discernment.[8] There is good news too for those of us who are more extrovert: some of the greatest out-front leaders have been encouragers.

Pause for Thought

In what ways do you think the gift of encouragement overlaps with other gifts?

My Approach in This Study

In this booklet I am presenting the indivisible ministry of encouragement as three dynamics: strengthening *presence, words* of comfort and challenge and the giving of *gifts*—and all in the context of *community*.

Each chapter explores one of these aspects of encouragement through stories from life, an introduction to some of the sons and daughters of encouragement in Christian history, some biblical passages to engage with and ponder and some questions to think about and discuss.

The poetic reflections at the end of each chapter were first published as part of a doctoral study in which the power of encouragement was revealed in various ways as my research participants told their stories.[9] I hope you find them helpful as you reflect on God's encouragement to you and ways of passing it on.

Reflection

Sometimes we can feel that our lives are at a low ebb. For this minister of the gospel the experience of being loved in a Christian community changed everything.

Restoration

I did not think God wanted to use me.
It was a time of tears when life was hard.
The way ahead I simply could not see.
I lived my life emotionally on guard.

The praying, eating, laughing, having fun,
Being held, embraced, encouraged, strengthened, freed—
There was a restoration going on;
Team life a place of safety in my need.

Well Benedict for me he understood
The balance of uniqueness and being part;
The sharing of our stories—this is good!
Our spending time together healed my heart.

I came full circle in community.
Evangelist—God had a plan for me.

2 Strengthening Presence

Story

When We Are Stuck

I have four sons and on a family holiday quite a while ago we decided to climb the highest mountain in Ireland, Carrauntoohil. It was pouring with rain and visibility was not great. Halfway up all six of us came to a halt straddled across a slanted, slippery slab of rock (the path). 'I'm stuck,' said my wife, Karin. We all were: we could not work out how to go up or down. But our third son often seems to come up with an authoritative word of encouragement in tricky situations. 'You can do it, Mum.' And we did. At the top of Carrauntoohil is a huge cross which, as it loomed out of the fog, added another layer of encouragement—the strengthening presence of the symbol of the cross of Christ.

Pause for Thought

How have you experienced encouragement in a time of difficulty?

Sons and Daughters of Encouragement

In this section we are looking at encouragement as a *strengthening presence*. I think we could also describe this as the gift of *withness*, being *with* in a way that is transformative, imparting something that counteracts or displaces discouragement. Withness is a precious thing, and those who impart or foster withness are often perceived to be encouragers—in fact, God-like. Immanuel, God *with us*.

Withness

Mary and Elizabeth (Luke 1)

'Both John and Jesus are conceived in impossible circumstances: the one because his mother is too old and the other because his mother is too young and a virgin. One child had been yearned for, for years; the other not even thought about once. For one woman, conception is a blessing, marking her re-entry into a society that had despised her for her lack of children; for the other, conception is far from a blessing and carries with it the potential for exclusion from society for having a child outside marriage. The gulf that exists between Mary and Elizabeth is bridged as in one moment of mutual recognition each one finds *strength* in the *presence* of the other (my italics).'[10]

Theo van Gogh

Without Theo, no Vincent! Because it was Theo van Gogh's extraordinary encouragement that kept his brother afloat. It was Theo who believed in Vincent when nobody else did. 'My best friend,' said Vincent: 'More friends than brothers.'[11] When Vincent decided he wanted to become an artist, Theo offered to support him financially until he found his feet: A more business-minded man might not have done that. Theo linked him with other artists who admired his work…and Vincent began to paint stunning pictures. You cannnot put a price on encouragement!

J A Spurgeon and Susannah Spurgeon

Many people who appear strong up-front need a lot of encouragement behind the scenes. The extrovert-appearing Charles Haddon Spurgeon also had a hidden encourager in his brother. 'J A' faithfully cared for the detail of C H's many projects. 'Dear Brother,—I am not very demonstrative in gratitude…' said C H in a letter: 'I value you as God's best gift to me in this work.'[12] Susannah Spurgeon, although 'chronically unwell for most of her adult life…not only supported her famous husband in ministry, but also had a significant ministry of her own.'[13]

John Newton and William Cowper

John Newton was both neighbour and friend to William Cowper in his depression and they wrote extraordinary hymns together in Olney.[14] Newton's *Amazing Grace* is one of them. Another of the most well-known ones, written by Cowper, has probably suffered from its first two lines becoming a proverbial expression in English, but there is more—

> God moves in a mysterious way
> His wonders to perform;
> He plants his footsteps in the sea,
> And rides upon the storm…
>
> Ye fearful saints, fresh courage take,
> The clouds ye so much dread
> Are big with mercy, and shall break
> In blessings on your head…

This hymn is *about* encouragement, written *out of* encouragement received. 'All told, for twelve years the two friends walked through life together.'[15] This was an empathetic partnership. As Newton put it, 'When you pipe, I am ready to dance; and when you mourn, a cloud comes over my brow and a tear stands a-tiptoe in my eye.'[16] Over the next hundred years over half a million copies of their hymn collection went into circulation.

Brother Andrew

Brother Andrew, who founded *Open Doors*, found isolated and demoralized churches with persecuted believers who desperately needed encouragement. In Poland they said of Brother Andrew: 'Your being here is better than your ten best sermons.' In the Middle East, they said, 'Seeing him and his friends reminded us that we are neither forgotten nor alone.' A tribute on his death in 2022 recorded: 'His mission…was to encourage…'[17]

We can all find a way to be a strengthening presence:

> Spirit of the living God,
> make me be cool waters
> in someone else's parched land;
> a shady place, giving shelter;
> an ear, offering space to speak
> out the untold story;
> laughter for the weary,
> welcome for the wounded;
> empathy instead of sympathy
> to meet another's need
> rather than my own.[18]

Pause for Thought

Who are the encouragers in our lives—friends; brothers and sisters; parents and grandparents; sons and daughters; spouses; other family members; mentors, role models, pastors; team mates, colleagues?

Scriptural Engagement

Try reading these passages slowly, perhaps out loud, with pauses. How is the Spirit speaking through the text?

Jesus With Us—Luke 8.22-25

One day Jesus said to his disciples, 'Let us go over to the other side of the lake.' So they got into a boat and set out. As they sailed, he fell asleep. A squall came down on the lake, so that the boat was being swamped, and they were in great danger. The disciples went and woke him, saying, 'Master, Master, we're going to drown!' He got up and rebuked the wind and the raging waters; the storm subsided, and all was calm. 'Where is your faith?' he asked his disciples. In fear and amazement they asked one another, 'Who is this? He commands even the winds and the water, and they obey him.'

Luke 24.28-32

As they approached the village to which they were going, Jesus continued on as if he were going farther. But they urged him strongly, 'Stay with us, for it is nearly evening; the day is almost over.' So he went in to stay with them. When he was at the table with them, he took bread, gave thanks, broke it and began to give it to them. Then their eyes were opened and they recognized him, and he disappeared from their sight. They asked each other, 'Were not our hearts burning within us while he talked with us on the road and opened the Scriptures to us?'

> Jesus is the encourager who walks with us, just as he did on the Emmaus Road, walking alongside those discouraged ones, accompanying them all the way. Speaking words of truth and strength into their disillusionment, remaining with them, breaking bread with them, giving his very self to them. God the alongside one, our encourager, strengthener, comforter, counsellor…

John 14.16-17

And I will ask the Father, and he will give you another *advocate* to help you and be with you forever—the Spirit of truth. The world cannot accept him, because it neither sees him nor knows him. But you know him, for he lives with you and will be in you.

Strength, Peace and Growth—Acts 9.31

Then the church throughout Judea, Galilee and Samaria enjoyed a time of peace and was strengthened. Living in the fear of the Lord and encouraged by the Holy Spirit, it increased in numbers.

> Luke tells us that in the period following Saul's conversion and introduction by Barnabas to the apostles, the embryonic church enjoyed a time of peace. It was built up and replenished (Latin: *replebatur*) through the comfort (Greek: *paraklēsis*, Latin: *consolatio*) of the Holy Spirit. There was strength, peace and growth.

Comforter—2 Cor 1.3-7

Praise be to the God and Father of our Lord Jesus Christ, the Father of compassion and the God of all *comfort*, who *comforts* us in all our troubles, so that we can *comfort* those in any trouble with the *comfort* we ourselves receive from God. For just as we share abundantly in the sufferings of Christ, so also our *comfort* abounds through Christ. If we are distressed, it is for your *comfort* and salvation; if we are *comforted*, it is for your *comfort*, which produces in you patient endurance of the same sufferings we suffer. And our hope for you is firm, because we know that just as you share in our sufferings, so also you share in our *comfort*.

The word translated 'comfort' here is *paraklēsis* again: we encourage one another with the comfort by which we also have first been strengthened.

Pause for Thought

How have you experienced the encouragement of the risen Christ or the Holy Spirit in your own life?

Reflection

Can you think of a time when you felt the presence of God in a particular place?

A prayed-in church building can often be a place of encounter, a café (in the following poem the café is located in a crypt) a place of welcome. We go on our way refreshed, strengthened—

Sacred Space

Come light a candle, seek your sacred space—
Our arms are open, let us share your load;
Come sense the supernatural touch of grace
And leave the building with a bigger God.

The cryptic cafe speaks a word of warmth,
The team are here, mixed in, part of the scene;
We laugh together, drink each other's health—
The scent of hospitality is keen.

Our prayer: that God will bless these hallowed gates—
The people coming in and out of here;
A mission has emerged that resonates—
Our meeting and our greeting make it clear.

So touch, give ear, in fragrant space be found;
Come taste and see, enjoy your holy ground.

Words of Comfort and Challenge 3

Story

Blessing

When my first wife Karin died our four sons were a tower of strength. They all came from their homes to spend a week with me in Littleport. Of course that was a huge help with funeral arrangements, but it was the fact that they were together in the home, just as they had been as little children, that made all the difference. At her funeral our eldest son Geoff spoke from John 20 on 'weeping in the garden, joy in the garden.' Stu, Rob and Andy took their part, and other family and friends too. It was a powerful experience of shared consolation, just as we had all linked hands in a circle around her in the intensive care unit where she died and prayed over Karin words she had often prayed over us: 'The Lord bless you and keep you; the Lord make his face to shine upon you; the Lord turn his face towards you and give you peace' (Num 6.24–6).

Pause for Thought

'Blessed are those who mourn for, their strength having ebbed away, they will be replenished through God's own ways of ministering encouragement' [my own interpretation of the Greek *parakaleo* here in Matt 5.4].

How can we encourage one another in times of grief?

Sons and Daughters of Encouragement

There is a powerful link between the presence that strengthens and words that bring encouragement. The Christian story in every age and culture is full of powerful examples. Here are just a few of them.

Latimer and Ridley

Although the word *exhortation* may sound old-fashioned in today's world, its power when used effectively is undeniable. The Reformation martyrs Hugh Latimer and Nicholas Ridley are a famous example of Christians exhorting one another *in extremis*: 'Be of good comfort, Master Ridley, and play the man; we shall this day by God's grace light such a candle in England, as I trust shall never be put out.'[19] Note the mixture of comfort and challenge in these words of encouragement!

Elizabeth Fry

On the £5 note in circulation in Britain between 2002 and 2016 is a surprising scene. Elizabeth Fry is reading to a group of prisoners seated around her:

> She read that day the fifty-third chapter of Isaiah... '...All we like sheep have gone astray; we have turned every one to his own way; and the Lord has laid on him the iniquity of us all...' Never till then, and never since then, have I heard anyone read as Elizabeth Fry read that chapter... While she read, her mind seemed to be intensely absorbed in the passage of Scripture and in nothing else. She seemed to take to her own soul the words which she read and to apply them to herself; and then she raised her head and after another pause of silence, she spoke to the wretched women before her. Her address was short and so simple that it must have been intelligible to the capacities of her hearers...What struck me as remarkable in her speaking, and no doubt that which won its way so powerfully to the hearts of those abandoned women, was that she always seemed to class herself with them; she never said 'you' but 'us.'[20]

Hers was a ministry of encouragement. She was a strengthening presence who brought words of comfort and challenge. She became known as 'the angel of the prisons.'

Elizabeth Fry had a motto: 'I must work the works of him that sent me while it is day—night is coming' that appears in her journal as a centre for her life (John 9.4). During her younger years she received much encouragement through her family and in the Quaker community in Norwich, but still struggled to know if God was real. There were two particular times as a young adult when words of comfort and challenge were offered that changed her life—an *evangelistic* occasion and a *prophetic* moment.

In 1798 William Savery, an itinerant evangelist travelling in the ministry visited the Friends in Norwich, and young Elizabeth heard the Lord speaking through him. She wrote in her journal that this minister had 'something definite to say and great feeling in saying it...I have felt there is a God...He was a messenger of glad tidings.'[21] Her call to minister dated from this time, though she had little idea of what form this might take.

Later in the same year she received a further word of encouragement when another of the Friends, Deborah Darby, prophesied that Elizabeth would be 'Light to the blind, speech to the dumb, feet to the lame.' Elizabeth, who saw herself as a practical person rather than a visionary, was excited: she had been waiting for something to do and someone to help. And then it hit her: she would teach local children how to read, visit them in their homes, nurse them.[22]

Elizabeth Fry's ways of encouraging—and challenging!—led not only to prison reform in many countries but also eventually to the foundation of modern nursing: 'Later, Florence Nightingale would take Fry Nurses with her in the first band that went out to the Crimea.'[23]

Sir Winston Churchill

'I have nothing to offer but blood, toil, tears and sweat' is a strange sort of encouragement! Yet Churchill's unmistakable presence as Britain's prime minister in a time of severe national stress proved to be a source of encouragement to many. So where did his own encouragement come from? Churchill's childhood nanny, Elizabeth Everest, was a bright light in his unhappy childhood. She was the one person who took a real interest in him, and they remained friends until her death: 'I shall never know such a friend again,' Churchill wrote to his mother. Elizabeth Everest was a woman of prayer who helped him memorize his first Scriptures and, by all accounts, explained the world to him in simple but distinctly Christian terms: the Exodus and the Sermon on the Mount became part of his worldview. Jonathan Sandys and Wallace Henley in their book *God and Churchill* argue that this is why Churchill could 'inspire hope, call for strength and faith and, most importantly, grasp the true meaning of Nazism and its threat to civilization.'[24] He spoke words of encouragement to disheartened, frightened people.

William Carey and William Wilberforce

William Carey's tireless work led to some extraordinary reforms now embedded in modern India. He had a friend, John Newton, who in a letter encouraged him to persevere when he was ready to give up for lack of visible results. Carey wrote back to Newton, 'The justice of your remarks upon disappointments, and want of success, was such as struck me very forcibly, and contributed much to my support and *encouragement* (my italics) and I feel myself determined to go on…'[25] That letter must have contained something more than soft comfort!

When William Wilberforce felt overwhelmed by God's call on his life, he went to see John Newton. On more than one occasion Newton reminded Wilberforce that God had placed him in Parliament: 'May the wisdom that influenced Joseph and Moses and Daniel rest upon you…who knoweth but God has raised you up for such a time as this.'[26] The ministry of encouragement is so often also the ministry of blessing, including a focused challenge.

John Newton's effect on those he supported and exhorted was extraordinary. As well as his next-door neighbour Cowper, Wilberforce and the abolitionists, and Carey in India, his wise counsel led to Hannah More having the courage to employ her formidable literary talent in the cause of the gospel and for the welfare of society. Newton was also a hidden encourager of Charles Simeon of Cambridge, who encouraged Henry Martin and countless others. The ripples from Newton's ministry of encouragement have continued to this day.

Letters, poems, songs and hymns...written words can so often be a form of encouragement. A book may be written that provides much-needed encouragement to those who read it at the time or perhaps many years or even centuries later. Sometimes in the Cambridge University Library I come across a book in my research that no one appears to have read. It is pristine on the shelves and maybe it has been like that for years...'Pick it up and read it!' comes the ancient call—an encouragement lying in wait for me! Often it is a challenge to take to heart and act upon.[27]

Pause for Thought

Can you give an example of 'uncomfortable comfort' that turned out to be helpful—or even life-changing?

Scriptural Engagement

Ponder the following passages. What dimensions of encouragement are revealed?

Comfort—Isa 40.1-3 (AV)

Comfort ye, *comfort* ye my people, saith your God. Speak ye comfortably to Jerusalem, and cry unto her, that her warfare is accomplished, that her iniquity is pardoned: for she hath received of the LORD's hand double for all her sins. The voice of him that crieth in the wilderness, Prepare ye the way of the LORD, make straight in the desert a highway for our God.

One of the features of this passage that cannot be communicated in Modern English is the ringing opening cry. 'Comfort, O comfort my people' is a plural command, and not a singular one. God is not here telling his prophet to go and comfort his people. Instead the cry goes out 'Is there anyone out there who will comfort my people?' This whole passage begins with God searching for people to bring comfort and, not only that, also to speak 'to the heart of Jerusalem' (which is a more literal translation of the Hebrew than 'speak tenderly to Jerusalem'). The message spoken must speak to the very heart of the people; it will comfort their brokenness but also resonate truthfully, deep within them. Jerusalem, the place where God dwelt among the people, is to take comfort because God will return.[28]

A voice says 'Cry out!' (Isa 40.6). 'What shall I cry?' says the prophet. Many things! 'The Word of our God stands forever! Here is your God! He carries his lambs—us—close to his heart. He will not grow tired or weary. Those who hope in the Lord will renew their strength. Do not be afraid, O worm Jacob, O little Israel, for I myself will help you (Isaiah 41). A bruised reed he will not break (Isaiah 42). When you walk through the fire you will not be burned (Isaiah 43). I will pour out my Spirit on your offspring (Isaiah 44). I, the Lord, speak the truth (Isaiah 45). The comforter is speaking! On and on goes the voice of encouragement through Isaiah. Isaiah is the Bible's book of encouragement—both comforting and challenging.

Exhortation—2 Cor 5.20—6.2

We are therefore Christ's ambassadors, as though God were *making his appeal* through us. We implore you on Christ's behalf: Be reconciled to God…As God's co-workers we *urge* you not to receive God's grace in vain.

Pause for Thought

What do you think is the right balance between comfort and challenge when offering encouragement?

Reflection

How do listening and speaking go together in encouragement?

Words of encouragement to us when we are young can often be a resource later on. They may be the foundation for a vocation to support and strengthen others.

Shaped by Others

When I was washing up at SU camp
The Lord called me, 'I have a job for you—
To do the evening talk, hold out my lamp!'
Was terrified, did not know what to do.

But God the Holy Spirit held my hand.
They came to me and said, We think your talk
Was great, it really helped us understand!
(An infant leader learning how to walk…)

Our space is safe, the circle of our care
The burden of a heavy spirit lifts;
We're doing Life Together, Scripture, prayer,
Discovering each other's different gifts.

I'm learning to be open, though I'm 'chief'—
We're shaped by others, this is my belief.

4 Gifts to Give

Story

Hats Off to Uganda!

In 2024 my wife Alison and I found ourselves transporting 500 knitted hats (vacuum-packed in three suitcases) from the UK to a children's centre in Mbale, Uganda.[29] I had mentioned on social media and in a few conversations that we would be visiting a children's centre there, and perhaps there were those who would like to send a hat or two with us. I underestimated the response—knitting circles are communities of encouragement! Knitters in Cambridgeshire, Lincolnshire and other places got to work and the result was much joy in being part of a 'great collection' (Acts 11.29). There were so many hats to distribute that after visiting the children's centre we were asked to go into the adjacent neighbourhood to offer hats to the people we would meet. There were even enough hats for a cohort of young people in a local church and for premature babies in more than one hospital, all received with joy. Mission teamwork comes in all shapes and sizes: here it was intergenerational with (mainly) older folk knitting and (mainly) younger adults distributing. Church leaders in the UK were able to encourage folk that they were participating in mission by knitting (where Dorcas led the way in Acts 9?) and church leaders in Uganda were able to demonstrate links with the universal church beyond their locality in a tangible way. It all started with a surprise—the realization that woollen hats are very useful for rainy days and cold nights in Uganda—and ended as an unforgettable sign of God's kingdom. Encouragement all round!

Pause for Thought

Think of a gift you offered that was gratefully received. What difference did that make?

Sons and Daughters of Encouragement

The Gift of Assistance

In football an *assist* is when one player passes the ball to another in such a way that the second player has a great opportunity to score a goal. An assist is offering an unselfish gift. If you had kept the ball you might have scored the goal yourself, but football is a team game, just like encouragement. Pele, Brazil's all-time leading goal-scorer, also produced amazing assists. How wonderful it must have been to play with Pele, knowing that you could be given the gift of a ball to your feet so that you could score the goal for the team.

When I was a lad assists were not really mentioned in football, only goals scored. I think it is good that this has changed. But then again, we can all be encouragers in whatever position God has placed us: the unobtrusively brilliant midfielder who can turn defence into attack; or the defender who is completely unflappable; or the goalkeeper with those safe hands.

The Gift of Listening

How often do we really listen?

> Listening, which requires silence, is a substantial element in the language of paraclesis.[30]
>
> Christians, especially ministers, so often think they must always contribute something when they are in the company of others...They forget that listening can be a greater service than speaking.[31]
>
> In my personal experience...the companionship of a listening friend is essential for me to express my story, whether it is a story that needs a solution or a story that I simply need to tell because it is too painful to keep locked up. And this tells me much about our humanity...It is a sobering thought that there are parts of our society where people have no idea of what it is like to be listened to, and, because they are not listened to, they often have to resort to screaming and violence.[32]

The Ministry of Gift-spotting

It was Abbess Hilda of Whitby who discerned Caedmon's gift and encouraged him, spotted his vocation and nurtured it. Simon Reed takes up the story:

> Caedmon lived and worked as a cowherd in Hilda's great village of God at Whitby. A common feature of the culture of Celtic and Anglo-Saxon England was that in the evenings people would gather round the fire to take it in turns to sing songs and tell stories. Caedmon was a shy man and would always find an excuse to slip out when it came close to his turn to perform. One night he went back to mind the cattle and, having gone to sleep, he had a dream. God appeared to him in the form of a man and asked him to sing something. Caedmon made his usual excuses, but the visitor insisted and told him he must sing about God's creation. Caedmon burst spontaneously into song.

In the morning, not even he could keep this quiet for long and he was taken to Hilda, who listened carefully to his story. To test and develop his gift, she set him some homework. Caedmon was read a biblical story and told to come back with another song, which he duly did. Hilda instructed the monastic community to receive him as a full member and to teach him the Scriptures so that he could put them into songs and poems in English which ordinary people could understand.

We only have a fragment of that first song, known as 'Caedmon's Hymn':

> Now let me praise the keeper of Heaven's kingdom,
> The might of the Creator, and his thought,
> The work of the Father of glory, how each of wonders
> The Eternal Lord established in the beginning.
> He first created for the sons of men
> Heaven as a roof, the holy Creator,
> Then Middle-earth the keeper of mankind,
> The Eternal Lord, afterwards made,
> The earth for men, the Almighty Lord.

Scholars widely agree that this is the oldest written poem in the English language.[33]

Caedmon's response to the encouragement he received from God—both directly and through others—blesses us today.

Paracletic Lives

For some the language of generous giving may be their principal language of encouragement. They may not feel that words come easily. Their passionate hearts resonate with actions that speak louder than words. Giving happens in so many different ways.

There is such a thing as 'a paracletic life.'[34] In our lives we discover extraordinary people—those who give generously of the time they have been given, choosing to invest in the encouragement of others instead of putting their feet up. Unseen, they encourage the discouraged in their neighbourhoods, care for the carers, pray, work, give. For them it matters not what you call it—mercy, compassion, support, helping, giving—they just get on and do it, and bring far more encouragement than they could ever imagine. Their example of consistency is a treasure much sought. They scatter the darkness with the light that shines out through earthenware vessels, for that is the way God has planned it. Weak though we often feel, we can still comfort others with the comfort we ourselves have received.

We may even have the joy of discerning whole communities of encouragement where we are ministering.

Pause for Thought

Who in your local church or among your Christian friends do you think demonstrates a ministry of encouragement (whether they realize it or not)?

Scriptural Engagement

Ponder the following passages. Try to imagine what it was like being encouraged by Barnabas.

Acts 4.33-37—Barnabas Giving Money/Possessions

With great power the apostles continued to testify to the resurrection of the Lord Jesus. And God's grace was so powerfully at work in them all that there were no needy persons among them. For from time to time those who owned land or houses sold them, brought the money from the sales and put it at the apostles' feet, and it was distributed to anyone who had need. Joseph, a Levite from Cyprus, whom the apostles called Barnabas (which means 'son of *encouragement*'), sold a field he owned and brought the money and put it at the apostles' feet.

Acts 9.26-27—Barnabas and Bridge-building

When he came to Jerusalem, Saul tried to join the disciples, but they were all afraid of him, not believing that he really was a disciple. But Barnabas took him and brought him to the apostles. He told them how Saul on his journey had seen the Lord and that the Lord had spoken to him, and how in Damascus he had preached fearlessly in the name of Jesus.

Acts 11.21-26—Barnabas Giving Time and Attention

The Lord's hand was with them, and a great number of people believed and turned to the Lord. News of this reached the church in Jerusalem, and they sent Barnabas to Antioch. When he arrived and saw what the grace of God had done, he was glad and *encouraged* them all to remain true to the Lord with all their hearts. He was a good man, full of the Holy Spirit and faith, and a great number of people were brought to the Lord. Then Barnabas went to Tarsus to look for Saul, and when he found him, he brought him to Antioch. So for a whole year Barnabas and Saul met with the church and taught great numbers of people. The disciples were called Christians first at Antioch.

Acts 15.36-41—Barnabas Validating

Some time later Paul said to Barnabas, 'Let us go back and visit the believers in all the towns where we preached the word of the Lord and see how they are doing.' Barnabas wanted to take John, also called Mark, with them, but Paul did not think it wise to take him, because he had deserted them in Pamphylia and had not continued with them in the work. They had such a sharp disagreement that they parted company. Barnabas took Mark and sailed for Cyprus, but Paul chose Silas and left, commended by the believers to the grace of the Lord. He went through Syria and Cilicia, strengthening the churches.

Pause for Thought

Barnabas displayed generosity of heart, created space for others, spoke up for outsiders, built bridges, spotted gifts, gave of his time and possessions. What are the gifts of encouragement that each of us can offer?

Reflection

How can our gifts and ministries best be combined to make Christ known?

Combining giftings in a team is not straightforward, especially when there are a number of gifts of leadership. We need discernment, patience and most of all the gift of God's grace.

Clergy Team

Our team: one's level-headed, wise with people;
Another's very clever—strategist;
The third's enthusiastic, bouncy, cheerful,
While my role is to be the catalyst.

We join in prayer and planning once a week;
We're constantly in touch: 'Are you alright?'
It's not an over-closeness that we seek,
But space in life and team—we're not that tight.

The playing to our strengths a conscious plan—
We know our gifts are wonderfully contrasting;
This combination's drawing others in,
The good news of God's love communicating.

The way we go together as a team
Can either be a nightmare or a dream.

5 Communities of Encouragement

Story

Kindling Community

Brother Herbert Kaden, of Turvey Monastery near Bedford, was a Benedictine monk who was a great encouragement to me. I knew him for five years, having been introduced by a mutual friend. He died at the age of 101. 'Such a rich life—not in material possessions, far from it at times—but in love—there's no other word that sums it up, that constitutes this life so well-lived, that explains it: his ability that is to win and keep friends. It was a joy to watch initial meetings and see immediate contact: eye to eye, heart to heart; the other person feeling immediately accepted and known.'[35]

At the start of World War 2 Herbert and his mother had come to live in the city of refuge that is Cambridge and the idea came to me that I should drive him there for a day so that he could visit places that were dear to him. One of these was *Jimmy's*, a community of encouragement for homeless people located at Zion Baptist Church on East Road. 'I helped to start Jimmy's,' said Brother Herbert, 'but I've never been back.' We parked the car nearby and Herbert's eyes sparkled. I pressed the bell for entry. 'Brother Herbert helped to found Jimmy's—can we come in?' Once inside, Herbert was soon providing entertainment with tales of how he used to cycle from where he lived in Gilbert Road with a pan of soup in the bicycle basket. Rapport with the men was instant. As Herbert realized how far Jimmy's had come from such small beginnings he was almost overcome with emotion. His audience voiced their loud appreciation.

Pause for Thought

Brother Herbert, although officially in a community of just two monks, was able to create community through personal encounter. What qualities are needed for this?

Sons and Daughters of Encouragement

A community of encouragement is not easy to define and is probably best grasped through stories from life.

The storyline of *Call the Midwife*, a TV period drama set in the 1950s–1970s in London's East End, presents a mission team of midwives—some religious sisters and some not—who are discovering their co-working gifts and learning to accept and love one another as they offer both professional care and hospitality at the interface between mission and neighbourhood.[36] Their vocational practice, shared existence as a convent community and costly service on the road together are presented against a background of varied church, denominational and community traditions. The sisters and young trainees eat together, tell each other stories, care about each other's physical, emotional and social needs, and have fun together. Apprenticeship and mentoring relationships develop realistically over the series and surprise discoveries occur in every episode. The TV series is based on a midwife's journal of mission team living—experiences which were transformational for the author, Jennifer Worth: 'I started to read the gospels.'[37]

When I visited a friend in Norwich who ministers among the poorest in the city they told me their story of training to be a midwife in London. Their mentor had been one of the *Call the Midwife* community in its latter years and had experienced the strength of a Christian community of encouragement. Apparently, the TV series is not far off the mark as to what it was actually like. With Elizabeth Fry starting off in Norwich, this nursing chain of encouragement thus comes back, via London, in a circle—a thread which also includes the ministry of Edith Cavell of Norwich too.[38]

Isaiah 40: Comfort ye! 'The image is a little like passing on a baton in a relay race. God calls a message of comfort, and voice after voice picks it up until at last Jerusalem itself is commanded to speak it. What is remarkable about this is that Jerusalem, the recipient of the message of comfort, becomes the means for passing it on…the people must hear the message, grasp it, make it their own and pass it on. The comfort then, is passed on in a chain and is not left in a cul-de-sac; it is sent forwards….'[39]

How can we send forward the message of encouragement today? Jonathan Sacks laments a 'cultural climate change' and points out the calamitous consequences of an 'unprecedented experiment embarked on throughout the West' in the latter part of the twentieth century: '*the move from 'We' to 'I'*:[40] How can we recover a vision for the sort of encouragement that will strengthen what remains (Rev 3.2)? Where did we drop the baton? The Judaeo-Christian story of the people of God sets forth a call and a challenge to convey the message of God, with encouragement in all its dimensions, from community to community through time. The sons and daughters of encouragement from whom we have been learning in this study show us a way to do this.

When I arrived at Pembroke College, Cambridge as an undergraduate I had no idea of the golden thread of encouragement that linked this particular learning community with the Reformation. My college had been led by none other than Master Ridley, the one who went on to suffer death alongside Latimer. As tutors and students in Pembroke and other colleges encouraged one another to read and study the Bible with fresh eyes a spiritual tradition took root in Cambridge that has influenced the world in the centuries since. I unwittingly stepped into this powerful movement of student spirituality in 1978 and found myself drawn to Jesus Christ through the communities of encouragement I encountered.

My uncle, Gordon Silk, was from 1953 to 1964 a mission partner with CMS in Uganda, working at Busoga College, Mwiri. His letters to prayer partners and supporting churches in the UK reveal the joys—and stresses—of being part of overlapping communities of encouragement in Uganda—a school, a fellowship of families and a mission team for summer camps. In this team—sharing Jesus with some of the boys from the school in a deeper way—he felt especially at home, witnessing 'turning points in the lives of some.' In 2018 when I visited Uganda for the first time I met an ordained evangelist whose own mentor had been guided by my uncle as a youngster. Seeds had been sown, love shown, and something had grown.

For chains of encouragement such as these to continue into the future we need Barnabas-shaped leaders who are investing in others rather than themselves, who will be a strength and a presence when others are discouraged.

'If I look back at my life I discover that it was always someone else who set me on a new trajectory. I suspect the same is true for most people. Someone who was there when we needed it, who listened as we poured out our problems, who gave us the encouraging word when we were about to give up, who believed in us more than we believed in ourselves. Or maybe it was actually someone who looked us in the eye and told us the honest truth…'[41] Precious words of comfort and challenge.

What is our gift to give away? One Barnabas-shaped leader has been described as 'a facilitator…there to support and encourage not to form and direct.'[42] This leader, 'seeing future leadership in someone before others do…is not afraid to give away…Surely, part of an apostolic gift is to see the greater cause. That may be an obvious thing to say of any church leader, but history points to difficult transitions and even the break-up of movements where a leader has stayed too long.'[43]

Those called to build community as encouragers are embodying and enacting ministries of God the Holy Spirit, the encourager. This often involves costly 'go-betweening' as Barnabas did between Jerusalem and Antioch. This is the sacrificial activity of holy brokering and practical blessing of the sons and daughters of encouragement. It is the sort of ministry that builds, strengthens, maintains and restores the fragile bridges of human relationship. It listens, bears with, accompanies and sheds tears. It speaks the word of comfort and of challenge to those who may have given up. It gives and gives again. It goes out of its way to visit those experiencing discouragement. It brings hope. It dares the impossible in a fearful world.

Pause for Thought

Try filling in the gaps in these chains / golden threads of encouragement:

Without..no Paul;
Without..no Caedmon;
Without..no ministry to prisons;
Without..no Abolition movement;
Without..no Van Gogh paintings.

Scriptural Engagement

Encouragement in the Bible is in the plural! Ponder the following passages together. If you are reading this on your own, take a few moments to call to mind a Christian community you are part of (however small or large) and read the passages in 'imaginative together.'

2 Thess 2.16-17

May our Lord Jesus Christ himself and God our Father, who loved us and by his grace gave us eternal *encouragement* and good hope, *encourage* your hearts and strengthen you in every good deed and word.

Heb 3.13

But *encourage* one another daily, as long as it is called 'Today,' so that none of you may be hardened by sin's deceitfulness.

Heb 6.18-20

God did this so that, by two unchangeable things in which it is impossible for God to lie, we who have fled to take hold of the hope set before us may be greatly *encouraged*. We have this hope as an anchor for the soul, firm and secure. It enters the inner sanctuary behind the curtain, where our forerunner, Jesus, has entered on our behalf. He has become a high priest forever, in the order of Melchizedek.

Heb 10.24-25
And let us consider how we may spur one another on toward love and good deeds, not giving up meeting together, as some are in the habit of doing, but *encouraging* one another—and all the more as you see the day approaching.

Heb 12.5-6
And have you completely forgotten this word of encouragement that addresses you as a father addresses his son? It says, 'My son, do not make light of the Lord's discipline, and do not lose heart when he rebukes you, because the Lord disciplines the one he loves, and he chastens everyone he accepts as his son.

Pause for Thought

What are the 'threats' to being an encouraging community—gossiping, sharp criticism, competitiveness, negativity, lack of trust, controlling behaviour, other things—and how can these be overcome?

Reflection

Where are our communities of encouragement? Could we start one? Homes, church and church groups, neighbourhoods, leisure and interest groups, work, other groups and communities…

Dreaming of and then acting in faith to start a community of encouragement—here is one cameo of trust in God and intentional growth from small beginnings.

Candle, Table, Door

What did he want of us? We learnt to dream—
In presence of the Father, Son and Spirit;
We just sought God, together spending time
In Candle's guiding light. Now how to live it?

We started to build friendships round the Table—
The team became community one day;
We ate and prayed; we'd spied a holy gable—
The Barn—a home in sight! where we would stay.

And next a coffee shop, an open Door
Where people choose to come, and eat and drink,
Relearning being human, loving more—
The welcome in and sending out are linked.

Let's be prophetic in imagination,
Do Life Together with a shared devotion.

Notes

1 R Parker, *The Wild Spirit* (London: Triangle, 1997) p 62.
2 M Morgan, *John Newton: Catalyst for Compassion* (Littleton, CO: Acoma Press, 2019).
3 A D Opperman, *While It Is Yet Day* (Leominster: Orphans Publishing, 2015).
4 J Pollock, *The Billy Graham Story* (Grand Rapids, MI: Zondervan, 2003) p 157.
5 J Lucas, *There are No Ordinary People* (Farnham: CWR, 2015) p 41.
6 R Parker, *The Wild Spirit, op cit*, p 69.
7 T Gates Brown, *Spirit in the Writings of John*, quoted in E Richards and R James, *Misreading Scripture with Individualist Eyes* (Downers Grove, IL: InterVarsity Press, 2020) p 271.
8 E Peterson, *Practise Resurrection* (London: Hodder, 2010) pp 171–176.
9 I Silk, *Mission Team Life: transformative discipleship and leadership development in context* (University of Chester, 2021).
10 P Gooder, *The Meaning is in the Waiting* (London: Canterbury Press, 2008) p 90.
11 W Cook, 'How Vincent van Gogh's family kept his legacy alive,' *The Week* (25 March 2023).
12 P J Morden, *Communion with Christ and His People* (Eugene, OR: Pickwick, 2013) p 216.
13 C Heath-Whyte, *For Richer, For Poorer* (Leyland: 10Publishing, 2018) p 133.
14 P Seddon, *'And I shall see his face'* (Grove Spirituality booklet S127).
15 M Morgan, *John Newton, op cit*, p 46.
16 J Newton, *129 Letters*, 157–158, quoted in M Morgan, *John Newton, op cit*, p 47.
17 *Brother Andrew: God's Smuggler* (Witney: Open Doors, 2022) p 5–7.
18 R Parker, *The Wild Spirit, op cit*, p 70.
19 J Ridley, *Nicholas Ridley* (London: Longmans, 1957) p 418.
20 A D Opperman, *op cit*, p 218.
21 *ibid*, pp 24–32.
22 *ibid*, p 43.
23 *ibid*, p 300.
24 J Sandys and W Henley, *God and Churchill, op cit*, p 8.
25 Quoted in *Background for Prayer, Feb-Apr 2023* (Olney: The John Newton Project, 2023).
26 M Morgan, *John Newton, op cit*, p 87.
27 H Chadwick, *Saint Augustine: Confessions* (Oxford University Press, 1992) p 152.
28 P Gooder, *The Meaning is in the Waiting, op cit*, p 60.
29 jengauganda.org
30 E Peterson, *Practise Resurrection, op cit*, p 174.
31 D Bonhoeffer, *Life Together* (London: SCM, 1954) pp 75–76.
32 M Mitton, *A Heart To Listen* (Abingdon: BRF, 2010) pp 29–34.
33 S Reed, *Creating Community* (Abingdon: BRF, 2013) pp 64–65.
34 E Peterson, *op cit*, p 175.
35 J Mayhead, on the life of *Brother Herbert Kaden OSB* (Turvey: Monastery of Christ Our Saviour, 2022).
36 *Call the Midwife* (BBC1, 2012-present).
37 J Worth, *Call the Midwife* (London: Weidenfeld and Nicolson, 2008) p 319.
38 N Miller, *Edith Cavell: A Forgotten Heroine* (Grove Spirituality booklet S131).
39 P Gooder, *The Meaning is in the Waiting, op cit*, p 61.
40 J Sacks, *Morality* (London: Hodder, 2020) p 12.
41 *ibid*, p 39.
42 R Turner, *The Stuart Bell Story* (Malcolm Down, 2022) p 80.
43 *ibid*, p 171.